ART DECO NAPIER
Styles of the Thirties

Art Deco Napier
Styles of the Thirties

is one of a series of books about New Zealand's architectural heritage
published as
THE COSMOS COLLECTION

Other books in the series
by Peter Hallett and Peter Shaw include

SPANISH MISSION HASTINGS - STYLES OF FIVE DECADES
Published by Cosmos Publications 1991

WHITESTONE OAMARU - A VICTORIAN ARCHITECTURAL HERITAGE
Published by Craig Potton Publishing 1995

ART DECO NAPIER
Styles of the Thirties

Peter Shaw & Peter Hallett

ART DECO TRUST
Napier, New Zealand

PUBLISHED WITH THE SUPPORT OF
THE LION FOUNDATION

First Published by Reed Methuen 1987
ISBN 0 474002 51 9 (hard cover)

Second Edition published by Cosmos Publications 1990
ISBN 0 908887 00 0 (hard cover) ISBN 0 90887 01 9 (soft cover)

Third Edition published by Craig Potton Publishing 1994
ISBN 0 908802 21 8 (hard cover) ISBN 0 908802 22 6 (soft cover)

Fourth Edition published by Craig Potton Publishing 1998
ISBN 0 908802 45 5 (soft cover)

Fifth Edition published by the Art Deco Trust 2002
ISBN 0 9582030 6 7 (soft cover)

PHOTO ACKNOWLEDGEMENTS
Historical photographs were sourced from the Hawke's Bay Museum, the Alexander Turnbull Library,
Audrey McKelvie, Margaret Hay, the Santa Barbara Trust for Historic Preservation and Dennis Sharp Architects, London.
Archives New Zealand Photo: National Publicity Studios Photographic Collection, Alexander Turnbull Library, F17208 1/1 (5379)
Alexander Turnbull Library Photo: C24031 1/2, New Zealand Free Lance Collection

Book Design by Peter Hallett   Printed by Brebner Print Ltd, Napier, New Zealand

Published by the Art Deco Trust
Napier, New Zealand

Foreword

In 1982 publication of Heather Ives' *The Art Deco Architecture of Napier* by the Ministry of Works and Development began the rapid escalation of awareness and appreciation of Napier's unique buildings. In 1984 the Art Deco Group, now the Art Deco Trust, was formed to work for the preservation and promotion of what they believed to be an architectural collection of world importance, and subsequent events have proved them correct.

Today, visitors from many countries put Napier high on their list of places to see in New Zealand, and the attention the buildings receive has encouraged many of their owners to enhance or restore them and to feel pride in them. In this they have been encouraged by Napier City Council initiatives, in particular the Art Deco Improvement Grant Scheme and the imaginative redevelopment of Emerson Street as a mixed pedestrian and vehicle precinct which complements the inner city's character. The Art Deco Trust, in promoting the city and working with building owners and the Council to protect and enhance its architecture, has also played a major role in increasing both local and international awareness of Napier's architectural heritage.

Publication in 1987 of the First Edition of *Art Deco Napier - Styles of the Thirties*, by Peter Shaw and Peter Hallett, was a landmark in this process of recognition and appreciation, and the book has carried all over the world images of Napier's unique mix of styles which forms a tapestry in which all the threads of the Modern Movement are woven together.

For this fifth edition, a comprehensive update of the book has taken place. The text has been updated and the photographs rearranged so that the work or each architect is as far as possible grouped together. The buildings have been referred to by their original names, because some of them have been through several name changes, causing some confusion. The exceptions to that change are those buildings which have their present name clearly marked on them. And there are many new photographs, which record the love and care conferred upon the buildings of this small but stunning city since the first edition appeared. They do even greater justice to the visual delights of Napier.

ROBERT McGREGOR
Executive Director
Art Deco Trust

The Marine Parade c1900. The original Masonic Hotel
and the Boer War Memorial can be seen on the left.
The Band Rotunda is in the centre.

Acknowledgements

This book could never have been written without the help and cooperation of the many Napier people who cheerfully answered our questions and allowed us access to their homes and business premises.

No less important is the contribution of others who have written about Napier: Heather Ives with her pioneering book *The Art Deco Architecture of Napier* and Roy Blok, whose unpublished thesis *Salubrious Deco* is held in the Auckland University Library. Jeremy Salmond's *Old New Zealand Houses* provided an invaluable reference as did Geoff Conly's *The Shock of '31* and Dr M D N Campbell's *Story of Napier.*

Film maker Peter Wells was generous with information collected during research for his 1985 film *Newest City on the Globe!* Staff of the Hawke's Bay Museum, particularly librarian Annette Fairweather and her successor Gail Pope, were unfailingly helpful.

There is no doubt that awareness of the value of Napier's architectural heritage has greatly increased since 1987 when the first edition of this book appeared. This is outwardly demonstrated in the number of important buildings which have been restored, repainted or improved in other ways while at the same time maintaining their original character. This fifth edition illustrates some of these, replacing earlier photographs with more up to date ones.

The work of the Art Deco Trust has been crucial in increasing the architectural understanding of Napier's residents and visitors alike. Its guided tours of the central city's buildings are both popular and informative, its advice to building owners on colour schemes and associated matters is invaluable. The annual Art Deco Weekend brings the era to life, illustrating that the style is about more than just buildings. Its director, Robert McGregor, has contributed significantly to the text of this new edition of *Art Deco Napier* by generously contributing information that has come to light since the text was first written.

The positive lead taken by the Napier City Council in promoting a Heritage Area concept, preservation provisions in its new District Plan and proposals for the further improvement of the city continues to offer encouragement to all who strive for the preservation of Napier's magnificent legacy of the thirties.

Peter Shaw
Peter Hallett
October 2002

NAPIER
CITY CENTRE

N

1920s and 1930s buildings

SHAKESPEARE ROAD
(To Ahuriri 2kms)

BYRON STREET

HERSCHELL STREET

BROWNING STREET

MARINE

CHURCH LANE

HASTINGS

PARADE

TENNYSON STREET

STREET

EMERSON

STREET

DALTON STREET

CLIVE

SQUARE

DICKENS

STREET

STATION STREET

ART DECO NAPIER
Styles of the Thirties

The city of Napier, in New Zealand's Hawke's Bay, has long been renowned for its warm, sunny climate, its seaside location and its Marine Parade lined with Norfolk Island pines.

Advertisers used to call Napier 'The Nice of the Pacific', hoping to make their city sound as inviting as the French Mediterranean one did to English tourists in the 1870s. New Zealanders as well as foreign travellers journeyed to Napier to stay in its fine hotels, to swim in the famous Salt Water Baths, to stroll in the Botanic Gardens and to listen to the bands playing in the rotunda on Clive Square.

The town's very name called forth comfortingly imperial associations: Sir Charles Napier had defeated a huge Indian armed force at Meeanee near the city of Hyderabad, India, in 1843. When Alfred Domett was appointed Commissioner of Crown Lands and Resident Magistrate in 1854 he widened these military associations to include his favourite poetic ones. Having already used Clive, Hastings, Scinde and Havelock he decided that the streets should resound with the names of eminent contemporary men of literature and science. Thus they were named Carlyle, Emerson, Dickens, Thackeray, Tennyson, Browning, Faraday and Dalton. Byron, Shakespeare, Milton, Chaucer and Burns added their weight, too. This was necessary, Domett wrote in a letter, because:

> "... it is better to have pleasing associations with the names of our roads and ravines than to be constantly reminded of the existence of obscure individuals (ruffians possibly and runaway convicts) whose names get attached to the places they happen to be the first to pitch upon, and almost to render the places themselves distasteful, however favoured by nature."

Napier, already favoured, was thus rescued from distastefulness and by 1880 presented to the world the perfect image of an English seaside resort.

These Edwardian buildings in Browning Street indicate the quality of Napier's pre-earthquake architecture.

The Masonic Hotel and band rotunda were the scene of the big send-off in 1900 for troops going to South Africa. One year later, Queen Victoria's Memorial Service was conducted from the same spot.

Hawke's Bay's prosperity in the two decades before the turn of the century could be seen at a glance. Large public buildings, extravagantly decorated with cast iron or moulded concrete, lined the streets. The much-photographed three-storeyed Masonic Hotel was the favourite place to stay. Its tiered balconies were hung with people and signs proclaiming GOD BLESS OUR TROOPS and FOR QUEEN AND COUNTRY on the occasion of the town's farewell to its sons leaving for the South African - British War in 1900. They were there again the following year to celebrate the coronation of Edward VII, and again in 1910 for the visit of the Duke and Duchess of York. The architecture and layout of Napier were ideally designed for such grand social occasions.

The growing demand for more impressive buildings provided work for an English architect, Robert Lamb, who had originally come to Napier on account of ill health. Among other things, he designed a Marine Parade frontage very much along the lines of the English south coast city of Brighton. Although his designs were never built, they show that the image of Napier as an English seaside town was in the forefront of people's minds. It was also in the mind of whoever wrote the Hawke's Bay Motor Company's 1912 *Guide to Napier*, describing "the arrival in summer of families who came from the back country to seek the cooling breezes of the Pacific and a delicious plunge in the bright salt waves."

Visitors still enjoy all the pleasures available to the Victorian traveller in Napier, but the city now has a significant new claim to fame - its unique mixture of architectural styles. In fact few of the structures that graced the Victorian town by the sea remain; today Napier presents quite a different face to its visitors. The English-inspired colonial buildings have mostly disappeared and the modern city has a distinctly Californian appearance. It has been called 'The Art Deco Capital of the World' - an exaggeration, but not altogether inappropriate.

Tuesday, 3 February 1931, was a disastrous day for the seaside town. It was hot and dry at a quarter to eleven in the morning - "real earthquake weather," as they still say - when suddenly the earth started to sway violently. After a pause a terrific downward moving twist was felt, followed by the same swaying motion. In just two and a half minutes Napier crumbled to ruins.

Then a brisk easterly wind sprang up, spreading flames from the fires in two chemists' shops, one in Hastings Street and the other at the back of the Masonic Hotel. Because the earthquake had destroyed almost all of the town's water pipes,

Napier from the sea, on the afternoon of 3 February, 1931.

the fire brigade's efforts were severely hampered. Although buildings on the fringes of the business area survived, by next morning only a few of those in the centre remained standing.

The earthquake registered 7.8 on the Richter scale and 162 people lost their lives, a high proportion of them killed by masonry falling from buildings decorated with overhanging ornamental parapets and pediments. Evacuation began on 4 February when the Mayor of Palmerston North notified the hastily-formed Napier Citizens' Control Committee that his borough's Relief Centre could take 5,000 refugees. Women and children went immediately, men were expected to stay.

The town's water reservoir had fallen across the croquet lawn in Thompson Road, drenching the players, so 400-gallon tanks mounted on lorries were filled from artesian wells in McLean Park. Barrels located at prominent places were kept filled for householders who collected water in jugs and buckets. Sewerage was a major problem, electricity less so. After two steel transmission towers had been repaired, Napier received power from Waikaremoana the weekend after the earthquake.

Above: A scene of utter devastation – looking northeast from the Holiday Hotel on the corner of Hastings and Dickens Streets.

Bottom: In the centre of Napier after the earthquake – the Public Trust Office at right was one of the few buildings still standing.

Rushed immediately to the scene, a special reporter from *The Dominion*, Wellington, told his story:

> "Shrouded with a pall of evil-smelling smoke, Napier has become overnight a skeleton of its former self and the grave of what remains an indeterminate number of its population of 20,000 persons. With one gigantic sweep the earthquake has reduced the whole town to a heap of ruins, still blazing and crumbling at each shake. The population has become a community without a home, without food and water, and for the most part without shelter. In one moment, so sudden was the visitation, the population was divorced from its town to become, as it were, a thing apart from the mass of buildings that joined in one great conflagration from end to end of the business area. Napier as a town has become wiped off the map. Today it is a heap of smouldering ruins, the sepulchre of a prosperous port and the gaunt remains of a beautiful seaside town."

The Rehabilitation Committee worked with the Earthquake Relief Committee to organise the reoccupation of damaged houses. Each had one chimney repaired free of charge, but many owners felt understandably reluctant to reoccupy as the succession of aftershocks continued in the weeks after 3 February. Lists of tent dwellers in Nelson Park were made, their homes checked and gentle persuasion applied to encourage them to return.

After one enterprising shopkeeper put up the first 'Business as Usual' sign there was a rush to resume commercial activity. By Tuesday 10 February the Prime Minister, Mr Forbes, and his Cabinet were in Napier to see for themselves. Fifty Members of Parliament came on a special overnight train on 1 March, while the Governor-General, Lord Bledisloe, and his wife arrived by special vice-regal railcar on the 7th.

As a result of their observations the Government announced a loan of £10,000 for the building of 54 temporary business premises in Clive Square and Memorial Square.

'Tin Town' opened on 16 March. The first temporary building to appear after the earthquake was the Fletcher Construction Company's office block for 'Associated Banks', in which an unusual association of rival banks was temporarily established. After five weeks the Control Committee was disbanded and the former Napier Borough Council's functions transferred to a Government Commission of two men:

'Tin Town' - temporary shops erected in Clive and Memorial Squares.

John S Barton, a magistrate, and Lachlan B Campbell, inspecting engineer to the Public Works Department.

Because the Napier earthquake occurred when the world-wide Great Depression was beginning to be felt in New Zealand, the Government grant only amounted to one fifth of the estimated losses in Napier. Requests for loans to enable rebuilding were dealt with by the Rehabilitation Committee, which insisted that all national and international firms, banks, insurance companies and mercantile houses finance their own reconstruction. For the others, loans were granted interest-free for periods of one to three years, after which borrowers paid 4.5%. Many found this a heavy burden as they were already paying off pre-earthquake mortgages.

When the two Commissioners turned their attention to the central business district they consulted the Napier Reconstruction Committee. This had been formed in July 1931, meeting in the Trocadero Tearooms, Hastings Street, to deal with all matters pertaining to architectural design, street widening, town planning and building location.

The widening of the town's main thoroughfare, Emerson Street, had started before the earthquake, after property owners agreed to allow three metres to be taken from their land. Now the Committee added Tennyson, Thackeray and Waghorne Streets and Church Lane to the widening programme. All street corners were to be splayed, power and telephone lines put underground, storm-water and sewer lines placed under footpaths, service lanes behind shops and dividing the inner-city blocks created, verandahs suspended rather than supported by posts, and verandah depths made uniform.

The Napier Reconstruction Committee got through a vast amount of business. It dealt with crucial issues of public health such as hospital rebuilding, clearing of debris using unemployed labour and building inspection. It found time, on 22 July 1931, to depute to Mr H Anderson (of the Business and Property Owners Association) and Mr M S Spence (representing local accountants), the task of "drawing up a letter to Mr Rockefeller, congratulating him upon reaching such an advanced age and forwarding particulars, accompanied by pictures depicting the damage done to Napier by the earthquake. It is hoped by this means to enlist his practical sympathy." It also entered into lengthy discussions about the future of the Marine Parade foreshore. The inevitable sub-committee was formed to consider possible improvements.

The Napier Reconstruction Committee.
Back: A Mayne, A B Hurst, P W Peters, H Anderson, R M Chadwick, K McLeay, L Hay. *Front:* T M Geddis, Dr Fitzgerald, W G Martin, M S Spence, L Pickering, M R Grant.

Looking along the rebuilt Tennyson Street. At left, the Sainsbury, Logan & Williams Building is complete. Across the road from left, so are the Masonic Hotel and Market Reserve Building, although scaffolding still surrounds Bowman's Building and the Kaiapoi Woollen Mills Building.

The new Marine Parade gardens.

The image of Napier as an English seaside resort did not entirely crumble in 1931 with the town's buildings. The Napier-born but London-trained architect Stanley Natusch, although long an advocate of street widening, believed that there was little need for radical change to the essential appearance of the central business district. "The original town plan of Napier was quite sound and on reasonably good lines" he later observed cautiously in the *New Zealand Institute of Architects Journal* of April 1933.

As a member of the Marine Parade Subcommittee he also favoured the idea, eventually adopted, of putting debris from demolished buildings along the seafront, creating a garden esplanade beneath the Norfolk Island pines. When an official of the Parks and Gardens Department objected that aggressive salt-laden winds would quickly destroy the plants, Natusch's reply was simple and typical: "Remember Torquay!" - that English town being famous for its gardens.

The architect J A Louis Hay drew up plans for an elaborate Entertainment Centre and later designed a magnificent Albion Hotel for the Marine Parade. Alas, neither was ever built.

Hay provided liaison between the Reconstruction Committee, of which he was a foundation member, and the Associated Architects of Napier. Burying the rivalry usually found between different architectural practices, especially in small towns, the Associated Architects comprised C T Natusch and Sons, Finch & Westerholm, J A Louis Hay and E A Williams. The volume of work in the period of reconstruction was so great that it became necessary for these separate firms to operate as a design collective on some jobs. The Associated Architects also lobbied those in positions of power to ensure that local architects rather than outsiders got the jobs.

There was, of course, much discussion of the new Napier's appearance. On 4 February the Daily Telegraph reported that:

> "Napier has object lessons in other cities which have been laid waste by quake and fire and have been rebuilt to greater magnificence and grandeur than ever before. Napier people are determined that they will do the same."

In 1925 the Californian city of Santa Barbara had suffered a serious earthquake but had since been rebuilt in a predominantly Spanish style, as befitted its Hispanic origins. On 16 February the Daily Telegraph, under the headline *Buildings of a*

Uniform Style, proclaimed:

> "The attractiveness of Santa Barbara, one of the youngest yet most beautiful cities in California, is behind the suggestion that all permanent buildings erected in Napier of the future should conform to a uniform style of architecture. A handful of enthusiasts are working unobtrusively in the advancement of the proposal and have already succeeded in exciting and encouraging interest among architects in the city, who share the advocacy of the Spanish style of architecture, which is favoured for its multifarious advantages, notably economy, simplicity and safety."

La Arcada, Estada, Santa Barbara

Photographs and information arrived from Santa Barbara, which also appropriately shared with Napier a long, uninterrupted, tree-lined foreshore.

The talented American architect R A Lippincot, associate of Walter Burley Griffin and resident in Auckland since 1921, also supported the idea, agreeing that the elements of Santa Barbara's post-earthquake problems were identical with Napier's. "Santa Barbara", he observed, "instead of being a heterogeneous collection of unrelated buildings, each swearing at the other, has risen from her ruins."

By June 1931 a plan had appeared for the construction of one large building along Emerson Street, all the way from Hastings Street to Dalton Street, with an upper storey set ten feet back providing a Spanish-style arcade/boulevard along the length of the block. It never eventuated because, in the depressed economic climate, finance was not available to amalgamate titles, necessary to allow the creation of a uniform facade. But the Spanish Mission style is significantly represented in the Napier of today.

The modern appearance of the city is anything but uniform, despite the hopes of those in the forefront of reconstruction after the earthquake. Such was the urgency to get the town going again that there was no time for the protracted discussion of aesthetic matters required for the realisation of that dream.

But one thing is certain - the rebuilders of Napier in 1931, offered a clean slate, turned not to England for their inspiration but to America. Disaster had been visited unexpectedly upon their town but social ideals remained unchanged. In fact the alterations to Napier's town plan were merely cosmetic; no-one felt the need for drastic change despite the unique opportunity. The citizens of Napier wished to resurrect their town, not to revolutionise its appearance.

Similarities can be seen between these objects from the collection of the Hawke's Bay Museum and the decorative motifs used on Napier buildings.

Top: Art Deco jewellery.

Bottom: A Clarice Cliff 'Bizarre' tea set.

Napier, the Victorian town, had gone forever. England offered no inspiration in 1931, but the architectural journals from America were full of new and interesting ideas which Napier's architects were keen to adopt in the challenge of reconstructing their city. Louis Hay was already a fervent admirer of the great Chicago architect, Louis Sullivan (1856-1924) and of Frank Lloyd Wright (1869-1959). Some of the first graduates of the Auckland School of Architecture, grateful for an escape route from the dole queues, came straight to Napier, where they were given plenty of opportunity to work in the modern styles familiar to them from such widely-read American magazines as *Pencil Points* and *The Architectural Record.*

For these architects Napier was indeed, as Peter Wells' 1985 film so clearly showed, the 'Newest City on the Globe!' The city was to be modern in the American way, and that meant what we now know as Art Deco.

Writing in *Pencil Points* in December 1930, W Franklin Paris found the origins of the new style in a reaction against Art Nouveau, which was, he said,

"... cloyed with ornamentation based on botanical themes. Now in England, Belgium, France and Germany was dawning the realisation of a new beauty - the beauty of simplicity - the eyes rested gratefully on plain surfaces, well proportioned and logically disposed. In Germany industry allied itself to art. This cooperation, originating in Munich in 1907, bound together in a common effort some 800 craftsmen and manufacturers and resulted in the sensational exhibition of the Munich School held in Paris in 1910. Paris the year before had been agreeably shocked by the new colour values revealed by the Russian Ballet with its gorgeous settings by Leon Bakst."

This new modernist energy was dispersed by World War I, but revived again in the 1919 *Paris Exhibition of Decorative Arts.* Franklin Paris wrote:

"It was not until 1924 that the attention of the entire world found itself focused on Modern Art. In that year the French organised and held the International Exposition of Decorative Arts and definitely established the new doctrine. The Exposition made history. It was epochal in character and revolutionary in many of its effects. Its exhibits have been dispersed and its temporary structures demolished, but no-one can really understand the present trend without studying it in detail."

The 1925 Exhibition, *L'Exposition Internationale des Arts Decoratifs et Industriels Modernes*, was a lavish affair. Dominated by fine and detailed craftsmanship, it displayed objects and furnishings exquisitely wrought in ivory, Macassar ebony, silk brocade, Caucasian walnut, pale sycamore, chrome and opalescent glass. Today books on Art Deco style (the term did not exist in 1925) reproduce photographs of these dazzling objects with their stylised curves, geometrical ornamentation, primitive allusions and rich colour.

American designers in Paris for the Exposition took the new style back to New York and adapted it for their wealthy clients who wanted something exclusive, luxurious and modern. Others were determined to popularise the 'modernistic'. Department store buyers, fashion designers and decorators translated the new style into something more appropriate for the public purse and taste. As Martin Greif writes in his *Depression Modern*:

Clean lines and symmetrical decoration – looking south along Dalton Street towards the Hotel Central, 1933.

> "Characterised generally by zigzags and asymmetrical patterning, it reduced the wealth and endless variety of Art Deco to a handful of decorative motifs, a squiggle here, a stylised sunburst there.... By 1930 the modernistic filled the lobbies of New York hotels and skyscrapers."

The style we now call Art Deco changed further as the result of the constraints of the world-wide Depression. It became simpler, less extravagant, clean and uncluttered. Decoration on the predominantly large, flat, plain surfaces of buildings was reduced to bas-relief bands of incised abstract motifs frequently derived from plant forms.

American architectural magazines dispersed information about the modern style of building all over the world, including to New Zealand. In October 1929 *The Architectural Record* carried an article called 'Small Shops' by the designer J R Davidson. One year later an article entitled 'A Portfolio of Banks' appeared in the same magazine. "Similarities in treatment of exteriors, whether in this country or in Panama or South America, are readily apparent", wrote the Editor. The National City Bank of New York in Brooklyn, or another on the corner of 34th Street and 7th

The new Emerson Street, 1933.

The dining room of the Hotel Central, 1933.

The public office of the Daily Telegraph building, 1933.

Avenue, or indeed the Panama or Buenos Aires branches, could all be transported to Napier without any clash of style. This was an international style.

Napier's best Art Deco buildings are rather fewer in number than is generally believed, mainly because people have tended to describe the buildings in the whole of the city's central business district as Art Deco. But Spanish Mission-style work done by Finch & Westerholm is not Art Deco; neither are the Chicago School buildings designed by J A Louis Hay under the influence of Louis Sullivan and Frank Lloyd Wright.

However, the Hotel Central, designed by E A Williams for the Napier Brewery Company in 1931, has many classic Art Deco features. It was conceived as a solid block forming the corner of Emerson and Dalton Streets, the centre of which is a triple-bayed, octagonally arched balcony. The mouldings of each arch have been flattened and covered with a variety of geometrical patterns, among them the popular sunburst motif.

In bas-relief right around the top of the building, including the central bays, is the zigzag/chevron motif. This motif occurs again and again in Art Deco buildings the world over, but no-one is quite sure where it comes from. Many architects would have seen it used on Ely Jacques Kahn's Insurance Centre Building of 1926, in New York, but Kahn himself said that he borrowed the motif from textile patterns.

Inside, the same zigzag/chevron motif runs along the scotia, while faceted pillars are ornamented with the sharply broken up geometrical patterns to be found on the central bay's verandah. The architect has brought his external octagonal patterns and sunbursts indoors, weaving them into green, red and gold leadlight windows, skylights, banisters and doors.

Diagonally across the road lies the extraordinary Kidson's Corner, designed like the nearby Smith & Chambers Building, by Alfred Hill in 1932. It does not curve around the corner site, but moves in a series of flat planes decorated with zigzag as well as simple linear motifs which help to tie the various facets together. This building has been sympathetically painted, thus allowing its Art Deco features to be easily read from the street.

E A Williams also designed the Daily Telegraph Building in Tennyson Street. It, too, presents a symmetrical face to the street, again distinguished by a central bay which contains a balcony at first floor level and the main entrance doors at ground level. The zigzag appears around the entrance in raised wrought iron. The building's stripped classical symmetry is emphasised by pilasters placed at regular intervals across the facade, each capital decorated at the top with heavily stylised leaf forms. On spandrels between the pillars a small decorative motif subtly binds the whole structure together.

Originally the single-storeyed building was lit from above by leadlight and glass-block skylights enclosed within coffered spaces and decorated with bas-relief zigzag patterns. Today, with the addition of a mezzanine floor, the dramatic light effects of these incised patterns around the skylight, when viewed from far below, have been lost as the viewer is forced to stand much closer than the designer intended. But the planned (at the time of writing) restoration of the interior will enable what is probably Napier's finest Art Deco interior to be experienced once more as it was in 1932.

Then there is the Marine Parade's Masonic Hotel, built in 1932 to a design by the Wellington firm of Prouse & Wilson. It is an extremely simple, symmetrical concrete structure, enlivened only by its elaborate upper-storey wooden pergola facing the sea and its conspicuously Deco overhanging pediment above a suspended glass and metal verandah which proclaims the word 'Masonic' in Deco capitals of red leadlight. The building's long low-lying aspect is emphasised by incised parallel lines which run along above and below the set-in windows. The hotel's once splendid interior can still be appreciated as much of the fine Art Deco decorative plasterwork has been retained in modernising the restaurant and bar areas.

Standing outside in Herschell Street under the *pohutukawas* one can look along the facade and experience the illusion that the magnificent Temperance & General Building with its 'lighthouse' tower is part of the Masonic. This building was also designed in Wellington, by Atkin & Mitchell. Its stripped and undecorated curving form reached upwards to a tower, complete with Renaissance drum, dome and lantern. Instead of beckoning to ships at sea, the 'lighthouse' offers an illuminated clock to the citizens of Napier.

The image of the city building as a lighthouse had been seen in New York's Singer and Metropolitan Life buildings of 1899 and 1893. There is another 'lighthouse' on the path outside the the former Ministry of Works building, and another, even smaller, on the lawn of a house in Tom Parker Avenue, Marewa (*illustrated on page 85*).

Originally the building contained the T & G Insurance Company offices, leased office space and the Silver Slipper cabaret. Since its sale in the 1980s, it has been remodelled internally to house a restaurant and conference centre, but in 2002 it was

The Masonic Hotel on the Marine Parade, 1935.

The T&G Building with the Masonic Hotel visible at right, 1937.

converted into a boutique hotel. Two apartments will be built on the roof, an addition which has actually improved the appearance of the building from its best viewpoint, the north end of the Marine Parade. Original plasterwork inside has been replicated and the building contains one of Napier's two 1930s lifts, this one being the only example with its original decor.

Before the earthquake, the area between the sea and the Masonic Hotel formed the Victorian public square of Napier. After the band rotunda and the Masonic crumbled in 1931, the Boer War monument stood headless for seven years, the whereabouts of its missing part the subject of much enquiry. It mysteriously emerged from the banks of the old Tutaekuri riverbed during river-bank improvements in 1938, and the restored monument was moved to its present location, slightly north of its old position.

Across the road are three Memorial Arches designed by J T Watson to commemorate the new Napier and two of its citizens, Robert C Wright and Harold Latham. The Sound Shell, financed by a long-established local service organisation, the Thirty Thousand Club, is situated at the southern end, facing what was originally an "outdoor auditorium for dancing and skating", with inlaid Art Deco designs in the concrete surface.

The Soundshell and Skating Rink, late 1940s.

Louis Hay's grandiose Entertainment Centre was too expensive to build but Council and club funds contributed to the Sun Bay or Colonnade, where in later years the bell of *HMS Veronica* was hung to commemorate the invaluable work done by the ship's company in the aftermath of the earthquake. In 1990, after serious deterioration caused by rusting of the reinforcing steel, placed too close to the surface of the concrete, the Sun Bay was demolished and completely rebuilt to the original design.

Sound Shells were another expression of that Art Deco fixation, the sunburst. First created by Samuel L Rothafel as a form for theatrical performances, his Sound Shells were designed as a series of consecutive plaster semicircles. In the case of New York's famous Radio City Music Hall, these were painted gold to reflect the colours of the lights, but Napier's was constructed of stained timber for acoustic reasons. It was first painted in the 1960s.

In commemoration of the invaluable help given by the crew of *HMS Veronica* in the days immediately following the earthquake, the Ship's Bell was installed on the Colonnade in 1935.

Further along the gardens is the fountain presented to the city in 1936 by Tom Parker, a local men's outfitter. He had been to the English seaside town of Bournemouth, where he particularly enjoyed the play of a similar illuminated fountain in which colour and spray flow were interestingly varied.

Mention must be made of the magnificent Bank of New Zealand Building on the corner of Hastings and Emerson Streets, now occupied by the ASB Bank. Originally designed by the Wellington firm of Crichton, McKay & Haughton in 1932, it has many typical Art Deco features on its exterior. The stripped facade is decorated with incised panels featuring not the usual Art Deco motifs but designs drawn from Maori art. This building has been tattooed - a veritable Bank of Aotearoa!

Its designers exploited the obvious similarity between the Art Deco zigzag and a *kowhaiwhai* pattern on the lintels above the main entrance and borrowed from a carving pattern a motif used at the tops of the pilasters. The Maori influence continues in the interior of the bank where a *kowhaiwhai* decorates cornices and panels around the superb coffered ceiling's skylights. A mask from the head of a *taiaha* gazes down at the bank's customers from the main corners - the use of Maori motifs throughout the building underlines the essential New Zealand quality of the bank.

The Bank of New Zealand, 1932.

The one-storeyed Ross & Glendenning building in Cathedral Lane also has a frieze derived from a rafter pattern based on the *pitau* or fern frond. The use of motifs drawn from earlier cultures as diverse as Egyptian and pre-Columbian was an important characteristic of Art Deco design from 1925 onwards, and Napier's four Maori-decorated structures are well within that tradition of assimilating the primitive into the modern.

Louis Hay's original prize-winning design for the Municipal Theatre in Tennyson Street was rejected as too expensive after lengthy and acrimonious debate, and the present structure wasn't opened until 1938. It is the work of J T Watson, the City Architect. Severely criticised in the 1950s for its practical shortcomings and for its "regrettable aesthetics", it remained unchanged until the 1990s when a major upgrade took place. The backstage facilities and stage construction were largely rebuilt, a new foyer added to augment the quite inadequate original, and the auditorium altered to meet modern acoustic, fire and egress requirements. Fortunately, by that time, the regrettable aesthetics were held in high regard.

The building is an extraordinary blend of decorative influences which nonetheless combine into a pleasing whole. On the street, two squat distinctly Egyptian-looking pillars divide the three sets of double doors. When these are closed, the metal handles make a neat geometric pattern against the glass and stained wood. The

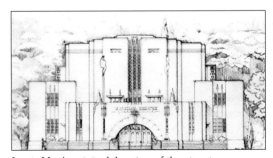

Louis Hay's original drawing of the street elevation of his proposed design for the Municipal Theatre.

foyer, lit with coloured glass lights, reflects the strongly favoured mechanical analogy which was such an important part of the Art Deco visual aesthetic. A curved walnut-veneered ticket-box, chrome strips decorating the front of the circle and wall lights extending out of chrome strips give the interior more than a hint of the 'streamlined' Deco rarely found in Napier, but which is a feature of cinemas in some other New Zealand cities.

The auditorium is floodlit by variously coloured lights cast from an elaborate central dome. Above the two side-exit doors, large symmetrically-shaped arched panels depict a leaping naked woman whose drapery forms a swirling pattern. This dancing woman was a very popular image of the time, cast in anything from bronze to plastic, and could be found on lamp stands, cigarette cases and clocks. Art Deco was, among other things, concerned with movement, with what the Futurist architectural manifesto called "a taste for light, practical forms, for the provisional, for rapidity." This interest in the mobile and the dynamic encompassed both natural and mechanical qualities; many of the stripped-back, smooth or aggressively angular forms of Art Deco buildings owe their appearance to the shapes of machine forms. During the Depression there wasn't the money in Napier to permit elaborate expression of these characteristic forms, but part of the city's uniqueness lies in the small-scale versions of styles more grandly realised overseas.

To call Napier an Art Deco city is merely to give a convenient label to a city which contains the buildings of an architect whose work draws on a whole range of styles quite different from those which have their origin in the Paris Exhibition of 1925.

J A Louis Hay (1881-1948) was a man of wide interests and accomplishments, a fine flautist, water skier, boat builder, sailor and actor. He remains in the memory of many who knew him as a genial fellow, though capable of stern decisions when the occasion demanded. He is still remembered for his treatment of those builders who tried, but failed, to get away with shoddy workmanship.

Hay's earliest work in Napier dates from 1911 and was mostly domestic. Very few of these houses were destroyed in the earthquake

Waiohika (1920), north of Gisborne, is Louis Hay's largest house.

Hay's presentation drawing of the never-built Albion Hotel.

because most of them were situated on the solid rock of the Napier hill or outside Napier, as far south as Hatuma, near Waipukurau, and because they were mostly constructed of timber. All show considerable influence from the English Arts and Crafts movement, particularly the work of Voysey, Lethaby and Baillie Scott. The enormous 7,500 square foot Frank Lloyd Wright-style house *Waiohika* (1920) outside Gisborne is Hay's most distant building.

Hay owned the two large portfolios of Frank Lloyd Wright's early Chicago buildings published by Wasmuth of Berlin in 1910 and 1911. These were to remain a lifelong inspiration to him, although his greatest Frank Lloyd Wright-inspired building, the opulent 1933 Albion Hotel, was never completed. The architect's repeated efforts to interest brewery companies in both Australia and New Zealand met with no success.

Another house, *Mornington*, in Sealy Road, displays all the typical elements of Hay's California bungalow style. Built in 1921 for Mr John Walker Findlay, the house is named after the Dunedin suburb where the owner was born.

Mornington shares with most of Hay's houses on the hill a long low profile, a preference for casement windows and pergola verandahs, exposed rock construction, and a low wide eaves line to give shade from the bright Napier sun. This latter feature clearly derives from the American Prairie house, which flattened the more distinctively English high gable seen in the houses of Lutyens, Baillie Scott and C F A Voysey.

Two houses side by side in Fitzroy Road are fine examples of Hay's early work. Two young sisters, Mrs Lila Hannah and Miss Doris Dolbel, commissioned him, in 1914 and 1918 respectively, to design houses for them; the backs of both sections were connected by a tennis court.

The Hannah house exhibits the characteristic low horizontal line, though the main feature of the structure is a false arch-chimney form which acts as main entry and binds the two roof planes together. Many of Frank Lloyd Wright's Prairie houses have a central anchoring chimney form which also performs the function of firmly connecting the building to the ground. *Mornington* does this too, its hilly site requiring a huge amount of stone from the nearby Coote Road quarry.

The Dolbel house boasts a magnificent pergola-type stone verandah and, inside, red, white and blue geometric leadlights which Hay designed in clear emulation of Wright's work in the 1903 Susan Lawrence Dana house in Springfield, Illinois.

The Hannah house (1914) as it originally appeared before the verandah was enclosed and another storey added.

The imposing stone entrance to the Hannah house. These two photographs come from Louis Hay's own album.

This house was obviously a favourite of Hay's and he frequently borrowed from it details of roofing, verandah and fireplace construction as well as leadlight design. Increasingly, too, he favoured its more open-planned approach to room functions, using sliding doors to permit freer access from sitting to dining rooms.

Like Wright, Hay insisted on using the finest materials inside his houses. He usually specified heart rimu woodwork and invariably designed a scheme of leadlight windows to suit each individual client's tastes. These ranged in style from the most sinuous Art Nouveau floral forms to the severely geometric, clearly influenced by similar work of Frank Lloyd Wright.

Hay's commercial buildings are some of Napier's finest. In the central business district the AMP Building shows his abiding enthusiasm for the work of the great Chicago architect, Louis Sullivan. Built by W M Angus Limited, it is a steel-framed, two-storeyed structure designed to satisfy the new laws governing earthquake-resisting construction.

Here Louis Hay indulged many of his architectural enthusiasms, creating a beautifully unified structure out of a collection of different influences. Derived from Sullivan is the arched main entrance on Shakespeare Road, decorated with bunches of grapes combined with elaborate leafy motifs. The other door, originally that of the Queensland Insurance Company, is even more spectacular in conception. In contrast with the semi-circular one beside it, it is clearly derived from the step-like vertical structures of Mayan architecture which was such an important source of Art Deco ideas. Here, too, tendrils derived from plant forms are placed so as to clarify further the geometrical design of the whole door. Ornamental designs in moulded concrete on cornices above windows, running almost continuously around the parapet, are discreetly placed on large flat surface areas, as they are in Louis Hay's Hildebrandt's Building (1932) and on those which feature the Wright-derived jagged sculpted concrete patterns Hay so often used. From Wright's 1903 Larkin Building in Buffalo came the design of the wall bracket light fittings - sadly only two remain today, installed on either side of an upstairs reception counter.

Now the property of Callinicos Hayward, lawyers, the building has been painstakingly restored by its new owners to the original Hay plan, the work including re-siting the staircase to its original position and dismantling interior partitioning. Publicity given to this work whilst it was in progress led to some of the original doors

Louis Hay's own album of photographs of the newly constructed AMP Building in 1933 contains this image of the arcaded staircase alcove inside the Browning Street entrance. It can be compared with the 1993 restoration illustrated on page 68.

and other important items coming to light. These have been included in the building's restoration based on an examination of the architect's own photographs taken shortly after the building was opened in 1933.

While never aspiring to the extremes Wright went to in his 1920 Aline Barnsdall Hollyhock house in California, there is a close resemblance between Wright's concrete decoration and Hay's. Examples of these can be found on such buildings as the Munster and Tennyson Chambers (1932), designed by Louis Hay in conjunction with C T Natusch & Sons; Abbotts Building (1932) with J B Frame; and the 1931 Napier Fire Station, now the Deco Centre. The once sadly neglected little Ellison & Duncan Building at Ahuriri, which had been deprived of its street frontage and swallowed up into a cartage contractor's yard but has now been restored and moved to a new, highly visible location, is a particularly fine example.

Louis Hay's best known building is the National Tobacco Company office of 1932, known since the 1950s as Rothman's Building but in 2001 renamed, with its original bronze letters reinstated, by its owner, British American Tobacco Ltd. In this Hay employed the distinctly Sullivanesque scheme of placing an arch within a cube, in accordance with the wishes of his client, Mr Gerhard Husheer, that the building be simple in form, yet highly decorated.

Hay had already remodelled three houses at the end of Elizabeth Road on Bluff Hill for this wealthy client. He had had leadlight designs returned to him on the grounds that they weren't elaborate enough. The National Tobacco Company Building shows no such restraint, covered as it is with cleverly placed clumps of sculpted roses. On either side of the doors, carved by Walter Marquand of Hastings, the roses are combined with *raupo* into a pleasing but unlikely arrangement. "The two piers of the arch have recessed bands of green glazed tiles which were hidden by paint between the late 1950s and 1996, when the building was painted blue." Vine leaves and bunches of grapes also feature.

The interior of the National Tobacco Company offices in the 1930s.

The gleaming brasswork of the banisters, the rich woodwork of the doors, the ornate lamps and speckled marble foyer with its beautiful glass dome make this Napier's most luxurious post-earthquake building. The Depression was an irrelevance to Hay's client.

Although they are important in number and scale, Napier's Spanish-style buildings are often overlooked in the enthusiasm for the more obviously Art Deco structures. It is entirely appropriate that a city with a climate as warm and sunny as Napier's

These motor showrooms in Spanish Mission style for Anderson & Hansen Ltd. were designed by Louis Hay.

Also in the Spanish Mission style is Hyde's Building by Finch & Westerholm, 1932.

The State Cinema (1933), by Finch & Westerholm.

should include a Mediterranean element, albeit derived from the Spanish Mission style of California. This arose in California during the 1890s as the result of concern that the Spanish missions of the eighteenth century were in danger of collapsing completely.

The imagery for the twentieth-century revival of the Spanish Mission style derives from buildings such as the *Mission San Luis Rey de Francia* in San Diego County. Here were the espadana or curved parapet, the adobe look of white plaster or stucco, the vari-coloured tile work, the arches, the twisted columns. The first major building in the new style had been the Californian Building at the *World's Columbian Exposition* at Chicago in 1893. It was designed by the San Francisco architect

A Page Brown, and modelled after the missions of Santa Barbara and San Diego. All these elements, much illustrated in architectural periodicals of the late twenties and early thirties, transferred easily to Napier. While there was little need or money for the extravagant campanario, or bell tower, of the Spanish missions, E A Williams used this feature in miniature in his very few Spanish-style buildings such as the Napier Club.

The major exponent of the Spanish style in Napier was the firm of Finch & Westerholm, which designed the ABH Building as early as 1930, the C E Rogers Building (1932), the Provincial Hotel (1932), the now demolished UFS Dispensary (1931) and the State Cinema (1933) among others.

The Spanish style was also utilised by C T Natusch & Sons in their McGruer's Building (1932) and by E A Williams for his large-scale Criterion Hotel (1932) and also Harston's Building, which was built in 1930 and strengthened after the earthquake, with its original Spanish Mission facade replaced by a new design. Nearly all of these have a centrally placed group of three windows as in the Central Hotel, except that in the Spanish Mission-style buildings the windows are often separated by twisted columns. The plastered white surfaces are usually capped by tilted cordova terracotta half-tiles, where cornices would once have been.

Many Napier architectural firms employed students who had just graduated from the School of Architecture at Auckland University. The sheer volume of work done in the years 1931 and 1932 meant that tracing, measuring up, and drawing details, especially of decorative motifs, had to be delegated by the firms' principals. The very real contribution of these young men to the final appearance of Napier is frequently overlooked. To a large extent it was they who chose and then drew up the ornamentation for a particular facade. They knew the "modern look" and were pleased to have the opportunity of putting their newly-learned skills to immediate practical use.

Men such as F Kingwell Malcolm (who worked for both Finch & Westerholm and E A Williams at different times in the thirties), J Hall-Kenny, Arthur Marshall, Charles Corne, Arthur Milne, Euan Wainscott, Graham Fox, Charles Crookes, Wilfred Bedford and Leonard J Wolfe worked for long hours in the city's main architectural practices. Many of them went on to become prominent architects in cities all over New Zealand.

Kingwell Malcolm remembers that "Westy", as H A Westerholm was commonly known, was something of a slave-driver, happy to leave frieze work and matters of detailing to his draughtsmen. He might roughly sketch a particular pattern and then say "Have a go at something like that." The draughtsman's work would immediately be accepted if it was up to standard. Westerholm left for Australia in 1936, but Louis Hay, the Natusch brothers, E A Williams and Walter P Finch continued to practise in Napier.

Although the sudden destruction of Napier provided the town with the clean slate so desired by the European avant-garde, especially Le Corbusier (1887-1960), the local architects preferred less adventurous solutions. Certainly Le Corbusier's notions, many of them in sharp opposition to those decorative principles illustrated at the 1925 *Paris Exhibition of Decorative Arts*, were known in New Zealand. A summary of his book *Towards a New Architecture* had appeared in the *NZIA Journal* in late 1929, but it was not until a decade later that the so-called International Style had any impact at all in New Zealand.

In the thirties English Architects were encouraged and influenced by the great Bauhaus figures, Marcel Breuer (1902-1981) and Walter Gropius (1883-1969), during their periods of residence in that country. Among them were New Zealanders Amyas Connell of New Plymouth (1901-1980) and Basil Ward (1902-1976) of Napier, who had worked with Louis Hay from 1918 to 1920 and maintained a lifelong admiration of his work. Their partnership, Connell, Ward & Lucas, made a lasting impression on the English architectural scene in the 1930s.

Temple Gardens at Moor Park, Hertfordshire (1937), designed by Basil Ward for Connell, Ward & Lucas.

One building for a Mr Wilkinson, designed and built by W Atherfold in 1939, shows some evidence of familiarity with the cube-like unornamented solid forms favoured by these European architects. Its roofs and walls are flat, its windows flush with the wall surface and its Cathedral Lane location, next to the Ross & Glendenning Building, allows immediate comparison with another plain but finely articulated Art Deco building.

As a result of the earthquake's upthrust, 3200 hectares of dry land had been created in place of the former marshy lagoon. Napier's new suburb of Marewa ("gift from the sea") was developed after 1935 following a lease agreement between the Borough Council and the Harbour Board, which still owned the new land.

Marewa from the hill, photographed c1952. Two thirds of the houses in the foreground are in the Moderne style, although some have had pitched roofs added since then.

It is in this area that most of the city's so-called Moderne houses are found. Indeed, Tom Parker Avenue and the streets around it offer an astonishing number of variations on the style. In most of them a slightly inclined roof is concealed behind a parapet which runs unbroken across the front and around the sides. Although the Moderne house has its weatherboard variant, walls are usually stuccoed and the absolute flatness is often relieved by horizontal bands above or below windows. Decorative plaster motifs appear at corners, on chimneys, and above entrances and windows, in an attempt to counter that plainness so vigorously promoted by Le Corbusier. Once again, the zigzag, speed symbols and other geometrical motifs make an appearance.

The alternation of cube-like forms with 'hat-box' curves is perhaps the best-known feature of these Moderne houses. Simple casement windows sweep around the exterior curved stucco walls, giving a streamlined sense of spaciousness often contradicted by rather pokey interiors.

These houses without eaves encountered overheating problems and today some of them sport brightly coloured awnings in a variety of inappropriate materials. A similar problem also arose in the central business district, and even the magnificent simplicity of the Bank of New Zealand building was encased in the 1980s within an ugly metal-and-perspex verandah shield, later removed in a major restoration of the building by the ASB Bank.

The UFS Dispensary, by Finch & Westerholm (1932), was demolished in 1986.

However, the happily temporary fate of this Napier Deco masterpiece was not as bad as that of the two-storeyed UFS Dispensary, built in 1932 to a modest Spanish-style design by Finch & Westerholm. This building, demolished as recently as 1986 and replaced by a structure misguidedly described as "more Art Deco than the original", is a crucial loss. Such destruction of heritage should not be repeated, and it is worth noting by comparison the beneficial effect on the streetscape of the

Emerson Building where the original facade has been retained.

By January 1933 it was decided that the rebuilt city was ready to be shown off to New Zealand. A crowded calendar of events was planned for the New Napier Carnival Week and the hardships of the Depression were briefly forgotten.

Once again the Governor-General and Lady Bledisloe came to Napier for the Grand Procession on 21 January. Two hundred and fifty decorated vehicles took part; Charles Kingsford Smith flew over in his Southern Cross; the Napier Frivolity Minstrels, New Zealand's oldest performing arts group, played to thousands; a corrugated iron structure labelled "Ta-Ta Tin Town" clattered by.

A fortnight later the city's heads were bowed at a ceremony in memory of those who had died in the earthquake. A thanksgiving service was held at McLean Park where Commissioner Barton, described as "an amiable and gentle Mussolini" - words which at one time appeared quite complimentary - made one of his last speeches. The first meeting of the Napier Borough Council was held on May 15, 1933.

In the town most buildings proclaimed their newness through their date-bearing facades. Their architects, foreswearing a post-colonialist return to English styles, had looked to the United States to give their city an authentically modern appearance. The range of stylistic borrowings they made in those difficult years made Napier architecturally unique. "The City Beautiful" it was called in 1933 - and remains.

Top: The poster advertising the New Napier Carnival in January, 1933 – a time to celebrate the rebirth of the city.

Bottom: Audrey Hurst, Hilary Gifford and Winifred McCarthy with their decorated car after the New Napier Carnival procession.

The Market Reserve Building was designed by Stanley Natusch of Natusch & Sons for the Napier Borough Council, just before the earthquake. The drawings were completed by the Associated Architects and construction began in mid 1931, making it the first new post-earthquake building. Its handsome bronze windows were supplied the English manufacturers, Crittalls, for the same price as steel, as a gift to the city and to set a standard for the reconstruction.

One of Napier's premier Art Deco buildings the Hotel Central was designed by E A Williams in 1931. It stands at the main intersection of the city at the centre of Emerson Street. The exterior of the building was extensively renovated and redecorated in the 1980s when it was owned by Countrywide Bank, while the interior has been largely restored to its original state by its present owners.

Above: These details of the Hotel Central's balconies show many typical Art Deco features, with zigzags and sunbursts symmetrically balanced on an almost flat facade.

Left: An attractive pair of windows on the half-landing with fine leadlights in a complex geometrical pattern.

Facing page: Facing Page: The ceiling laylight of clear, textured glass, fitted in a geometrical design, provides daylight in the former dining room. Laylights of this type were a popular solution to the problem of the dark interior.

The classic Art Deco sunburst is used as a design feature on stair railings, doors and windows throughout the building.

Zigzags are used above the shop windows and on this radiator grille in the hotel's former lounge.

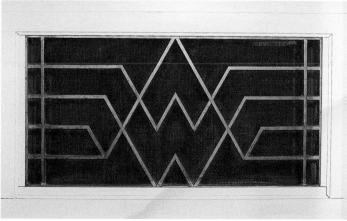

The Daily Telegraph building in Tennyson Street was designed by E A Williams in 1932. The most confident of Napier's Art Deco buildings, it also had one of the town's finest interiors – until a floor was inserted across the full-height reception area in the 1970s. But at the time of going to press this is being removed and the interior fully restored. The exterior colour scheme is based on the original tinted stucco finishes.

34

Above: This detail shows the decorative interior plasterwork at the top of one of the massive columns supporting the roof structure.

Right: The full extent of the decoration of the facade through the use of pilasters, the wrought iron balustrade and the timber doors with lantern-style lamps at either side, is clearly shown in this direct view.

Hawke's Bay Chambers in Emerson Street and Masson House in Dalton Street were both designed by E A Williams and completed in 1932.

Also designed by E A Williams in 1932, the Criterion Hotel has a Spanish facade.
A major fire in November 1990 destroyed the floor and roof of the building; fortunately
the remaining concrete structure was so robust that complete restoration was possible.

Facing Page: Even this fine Art Deco leadlight on the staircase survived the fire, against all odds.
Designed by Les Norwell, it evokes Napier's Marine Parade with a Norfolk pine, the sky and the sea.

Left: Left: Harston's Building was designed in the Spanish style in 1930. Although badly shaken by the earthquake, it was successfully 'caged' in 1931 and a new façade by E A Williams was constructed.

Facing page: Harston's Music Shop was known to Napier residents for sixty years. The building is now used for other purposes but the refined detailing of the shop front shown in this photograph, taken before the shop closed, has not been affected.

Below: Colenso Chambers in Tennyson Street (architect unknown), was originally the County Private Hotel. It has been converted to apartments.

The Ross & Glendenning building in Cathedral Lane was designed by E A Williams in 1932. Its simple facade is subtly decorated with an adaptation of a Maori rafter pattern based on the *pitau*, or fern frond.

PUBLIC TRUST OFFICE

The neo-classical Public Trust building not only
withstood the earthquake, but also escaped the
fire which afterwards swept through the ruins of
the city. It was designed by Eric Phillips of
Hastings in 1922.

The Masonic Hotel, designed by Prouse & Wilson of Wellington in 1932, was Napier's largest and finest post-earthquake hotel. It occupies a prominent site facing the Marine Parade and the seafront. Its upper floor projects over the street pavement, an unusual feature.

Pergola verandahs , another Mediterranean feature, were very much in vogue in sunny climates like Napier's.

The main entrance in Tennyson Street is protected from the weather by a glazed canopy (right) with the hotel's name in stylish cut glass. It is particularly effective at night (see facing page). The Masonic Hotel was the only post-1931 building with ornamented pediments – too many people had been killed during the earthquake by falling masonry from such features.

The T&G Building, designed by Atkin & Mitchell in 1936, was one of Napier's later reconstruction buildings. It is perhaps the city's most prominent landmark, providing the city with its town clock. The copper dome was originally stained green and its present colour scheme attempts to reproduce that effect. Now a hotel, following successive internal re-arrangements, it still retains some of its original features including its lift.

Top: Canning & Loudoun is one of only two remaining 1930s motor garages in Napier.

Bottom: This small office building for Richardson & Co in Ahuriri was designed by Natusch & Sons.

Right: The Government Buildings, later the Ministry of Works building and now privately owned and nameless, was designed by the Government Architect J T Mair in 1936, but not built until 1938. It's features a 'lighthouse tower'.

The New Napier Arch (1938/39) on the Marine Parade, like all of the 1930s architectural features on the seafront except the sundial, was designed by J T Watson, Borough Council Architect. Underneath these features lies the rubble of the buildings demolished by the earthquake.

Top: The Marine Parade lamps were first installed in 1930, and more were added after the earthquake. Identical lamps were used in Hastings.

Above: The Sun Bay, which has become known as the Veronica Sun Bay, and the Skating Rink were both built in 1934. The Sundial is by Louis Hay.

Right: The Tom Parker Fountain (1936) in the Marine Parade Gardens was closely modelled on one in Bournemouth, England.

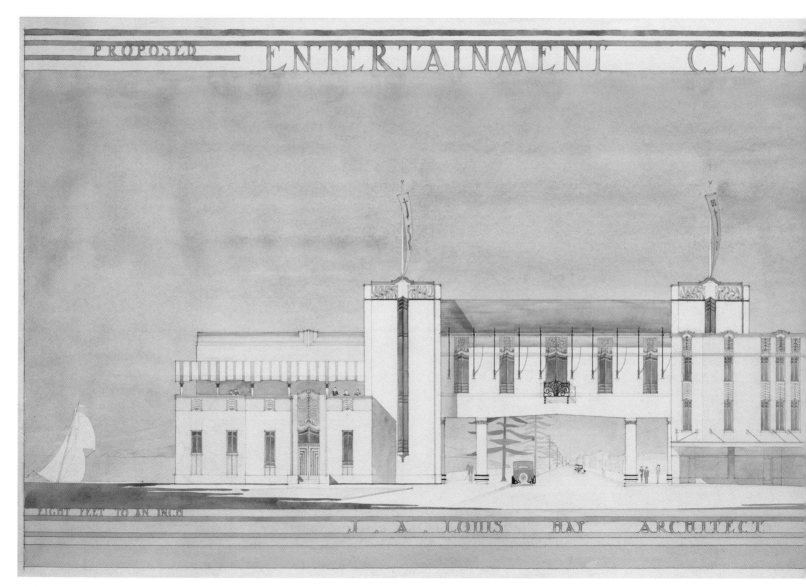

PROPOSED ENTERTAINMENT CEN[TRE]

EIGHT FEET TO AN INCH

J. A. LOUIS HAY ARCHITECT

48

Left: Louis Hay's ambitious Entertainment Centre spanning the Marine Parade was never built. Although large drawings of this scheme were prominently displayed for the citizens of Napier to admire, money was short and the project abandoned. This watercolour rendering is by Leonard Wolfe, who worked in Hay's office in 1933 - 34.

Above: J T Watson's more modest Sound Shell was built in 1935 on the site originally intended for the Entertainment Centre. In front of the Sound Shell, beyond the lawns visible in the photograph, is the old Skating Rink, intended as an "outdoor auditorium for skating and dancing", an area laid in coloured concrete slabs bordered by an Art Deco zigzag pattern. Uneven settlement of the slabs made the rink unusable for skating from the mid 1950s.

The Municipal Theatre was built in 1937 to the design of J T Watson, the Borough Architect. Louis Hay's prize-winning design for the architectural competition conducted by the Borough Council was rejected as being too expensive, yet the completed structure has many elaborate Art Deco features. The building was refurbished and considerably extended in the 1990s to provide a new, more spacious foyer and larger and more sophisticated stage and back-stage facilities.

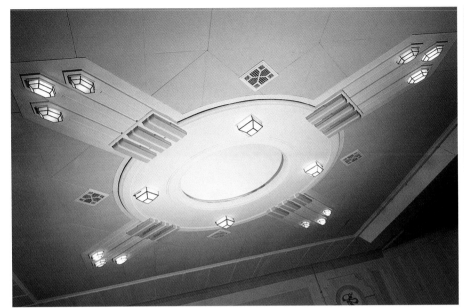

These photographs show the original main entrance with its Egyptian style columns and door lintels, the impressive ceiling of the auditorium, the spectacular neon ceiling lights in the original foyer and one of the two bas relief wall panels of a leaping female nude. The original cubist patterned carpet has been accurately reproduced.

A rich interpretation of the Spanish style, with twisted columns, laid 'cordova' roof tiles and curved parapets was chosen by architects Finch & Westerholm for the Provincial Hotel in 1932. An appealing leadlight window above the original bottle store entrance features wine glasses and carafes of red wine. The original fibrous plaster ceiling in the corner bar has been extended, using the original moulds, many of which are still held by the Hastings company which made many of the Napier ceilings in the 1930s.

Above: Finch & Westerholm also designed the State Cinema of 1933, again in Spanish style. The last of Napier's four 1930s cinemas to show films, it is now a retail premises.

Right: Another Finch & Westerholm design - the C E Rogers & Co building on Emerson Street of 1932.

Legal offices designed by Finch & Westerholm for Sainsbury Logan & Williams were described in the Daily Telegraph on their completion as being in the Italian Renaissance style. Cordova tiles on the parapet have been removed. The leadlight glass dome (*facing page*) in Sainsbury Logan & Williams, building is one of three in Napier, the most ornate being the one in the National Tobacco Company building.

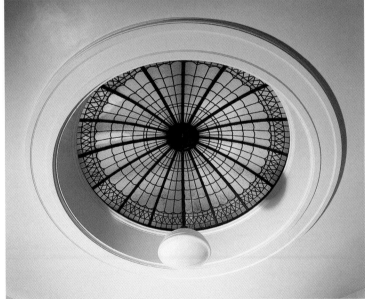

Top: The former Gaiety de Luxe Cinema in Dickens Street was reinstated in 1932, with a new façade in a Moorish influenced Spanish style.

Right: The Emerson Building was another of Finch & Westerholm,s Spanish Mission designs, almost all of this firm's buildings were in that style.

Top: This Art Deco motif brands the A B Hurst building in Emerson Street. Built in 1930, it was probably Napier,s first Art Deco building.

Above: Finch & Westerholm,s Shakespeare Hotel (originally the Empire Hotel) near the bottom of Shakespeare Road, was partly rebuilt in the 1920s after a fire and completed after the earthquake. Like the Masonic Hotel it has a Mediterranean pergola, this one on the roof.

Left: The County Hotel in Browning Street, formerly the offices of the Hawke's Bay County Council, became a boutique hotel in the mid 1990s. The corner block of 1908 was Napier's first reinforced concrete building and the building was extended in 1935. The upper floor was added in the 1950s.

The foundation stone of Louis Hay's Prairie Style 'Women's Rest' (now the Napier Community Centre) in Clive Square was laid by Governor General Sir Charles Fergusson in 1925. The building was damaged by the earthquake, but stood to form the core of the northern block of 'Tin Town'.

Louis Hay's home for Miss Doris Dolbel dates from 1918. The leadlights in the hall, although deceptively Art Deco in appearance, show the influence of Frank Lloyd Wright's window designs for his 1903 Dana house in Springfield, Illinois.

The hanging ceiling light looks remarkably similar to those designed by Californian architects Charles and Henry Greene in the 1900s.

Louis Hay designed *Mornington* in 1921. The massive foundations are of shell rock, from the Prison Quarry on the Napier hill.

In 1930 Louis Hay designed these windows for the home of Gerhard Husheer, founder of the National Tobacco Company. The leadlights are testimony to the skills of Douglas Pirie, who began work with Hay in 1926.

The unusual grille above the stair opening is closely modelled on a door design by the Italian architect Raimondo D'Aronco (1857-1932) for the Administration Building of the 1902 Turin Exhibition of Modern Decorative Arts.

TENNYSON CHAMBERS

Above: Tennyson Chambers was a collaboration between the offices of Natusch & Sons and Louis Hay, for the client was a friend of both. The exterior detailing is clearly Hay's work, with decoration similar to Frank Lloyd Wright's 1904 Unity Temple.

Left: Halsbury Chambers in Tennyson Street with its overlapping rectangles bears the mark of Louis Hay. Bowman,s Building (1932) is faced in brick, a finish used by Hay on three inner city buildings, however brick had no appeal for other Napier architects after its poor performance in the earthquake.

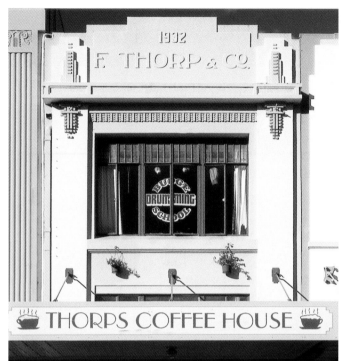

Above: Thorp's building of 1932, housing a well-known shoe store, was one of three in Hastings Street designed by Hay, all with similarities, in particular the 'eyebrow' which he frequently used.

Above right: Munster Chambers was another Natusch and Hay collaboration, for the same reason as for Tennyson Chambers. The clients were brothers, and of Irish extraction, which accounts for the shamrocks used as ornament.

Right: Hildebrandt's Building of 1932 was unusually restrained for Louis Hay. Originally coloured black and white, the origin of its unusual undulating wave and flag motifs is unclear, but the present owner has painted them to suit a local legend - that the design symbolises the German and New Zealand flags linked by the oceans.

Above: In 1994, Louis Hay's Ellison Duncan Building at Ahuriri stood in the way of a town house development. But in an unusual compromise, the façade was moved by crane to a new location where it has become a work of sculpture, adding to the streetscape in an increasingly interesting part of Napier.

Facing Page: Deco Centre was originally designed in red brick as the Napier Central Fire Station in 1921. Louis Hay reconditioned it in 1931, rebuilding the front portion in reinforced concrete but keeping the original design. Today it houses the shop, offices and visitor facilities of the Art Deco Trust.

Left: Two separate buildings providing Fire Officers' accommodation were added in 1931. Domestic in design, they incorporate appealing detailing.

The 1934 AMP Society building, now the legal offices of Callinicos Hayward, in which Louis Hay used elaborate floral motifs similar to those used by the great Chigago architect Louis Sullivan.

The complexity of Hay's fine detailing is clearly shown in these photographs. The sculpted group above the corner of the building was the work of F G F Mercer, a local craftsman. The AMP Society made use of this group on a number of their buildings throughout New Zealand.

Hay went to great lengths to ensure that the AMP Building's interior fittings matched its elegant exterior. These photographs show the arched enclosure of the staircase and one of the elaborate interior doors.

The hanging light fittings designed for the building are very similar to those in Frank Lloyd Wright's 1903 Larkin Building in Buffalo, USA.

CARE CENTRE

DEDICATED TO THE QUALITY OF SOUND HiFi GALLERY DEDICATED TO THE QUALITY OF SOUND

The Home Theatre Specialists

Above: Abbott's Building (1932) owes much of its decoration, as well as its long horizontal central window line, to the influence of Frank Lloyd Wright, particularly his Robie House, Chicago, of 1909. It was designed by Louis Hay and D B Frame.

Right: Details of the façade of the Self Help Shoppers Fair in Emerson Street (1932), and a Mayan inspired panel on Haynes Building in Hastings Street of the same year. Originally a butcher's premises, it is now the office of the Public Trust.

69

Left: Louis Hay's own offices in Herschell Street, built in 1932 to replace his earthquake damaged premises.

Facing Page, Right: Details of the Hawke's Bay Museum, designed by Louis Hay in completed in 1937 and 1938. The original entrance was converted to a loading dock in 1979.

Above and Right: Elaborate doors in the Museum are finely detailed. The exterior doors were moved to a new location in 1979, when the Century Theatre was added to the complex, and the interior doors are in the Bestall Gallery.

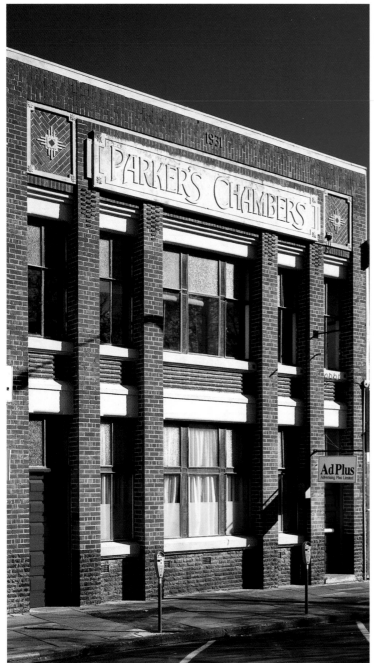

Left: Louis Hay designed a new three storey brick façade on Herschell Street for Parker's Chambers in 1930. The top floor was damaged in the earthquake but the lower two floors were quickly reinstated and bear the date 1931.

Above: The Hastings Street end of the building was completely demolished and rebuilt in 1932, with a contrasting design. All verandahs had to be suspended rather than supported by posts, so Hay fancifully designed metal supporting rods held in the mouths of lions.

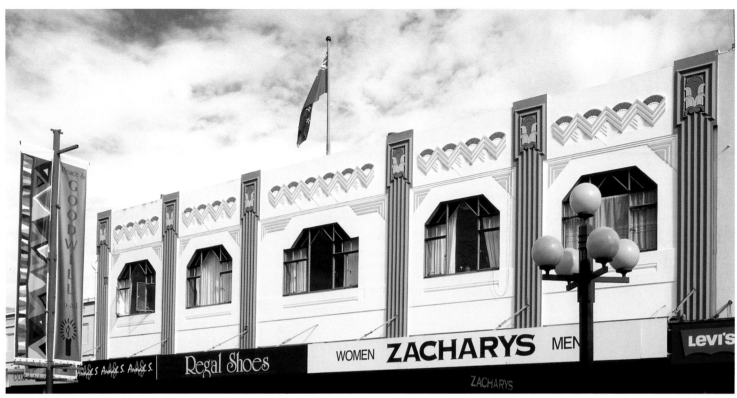

Above: These apartments on Emerson Street were designed by Alfred Hill. The decoration of the facade makes use of ornamental pilasters together with Art Deco motifs above the oddly shaped windows.

Right: Kidson's Corner building was also designed by Alfred Hill in 1932 and occupies a prominent site at the intersection of Emerson and Dalton Streets. It's unusually shaped frontage is the result of street widening. Buildings in Dalton Street which survived the earthquake made it necessary to widen the street on both sides, forming a dog-leg at this point. This appealing building features many classic Art Deco features and still retains its original shopfronts, altered in 2002 but carefully handled to maintain their integrity.

The ASB Bank, restored and refurbished in 1973, was originally built in 1932 as premises for the Bank of New Zealand. The design, by the Wellington partnership Crichton McKay & Haughton, makes great use of Maori motifs.

Above: On the lintel over the main entrance the similarity between the Art Deco zigzag and a Maori *kowhaiwhai* pattern has been exploited.

Above Right: This decoration has been repeated above the row of windows on the flank of the building.

Right: Inside a borrowed Maori carving motif tops the columns supporting the richly decorated ceiling. Another *kowhaiwhai* pattern adorns the panels surrounding the coffered skylights, while the mask of a *taiaha* looks down from the corners.

The National Tobacco Company was designed by Louis Hay in 1932. Here, no expense was spared. It is immaculately maintained by its present owner, the British American Tobacco Ltd.

The arched entrance was a device much used by Sullivan and Wright, as well as by contemporary English and Austrian architects. Hay exuberantly used a combination of sculpted plaster *raupo*, roses, sunbursts and bunches of fruit, in conjunction with polished wood, gleaming brass and mosaic tiles.

Inside the National Tobacco Company office the decor is enriched by polished marble and a domed skylight. The leadlights above the counter and in the exterior windows, which had been removed, have been remade from the original drawings.

The Hawke's Bay Harbour Board building, designed by
Davies & Phillips of Hastings with E A & L G Williams of
Napier, wasbuilt in 1940. It is in a typical 'cubist' style
popular at the end of the 1930s.

The Crown Hotel, in Ahuriri. It was designed by
E A Williams and displays some Spanish influence.

Top: This small office building for Richardson & Co in Ahuriri was designed by Natusch & Sons.

Right: Also in Ahuriri is the Union Hotel, designed by Edmund Anscombe of Wellington, who maintained an office in Hastings during the 1930s. Here again there are traces of Spanish features. The hotel was subject to extensive renovation and refurbishment in 2002.

In the 1930s Taradale was a borough, with its own council, but it is now a suburb of Napier. The Taradale Hotel and the Taradale Town Hall were its two major Art Deco buildings, both designed by E A Williams and built in 1932 to replace predecessors destroyed in the earthquake. Both have been altered to suit new requirements.

Above: The Taradale Hotel's 1996 conversion into a McDonald's Restaurant (known as the McDeco McDonald's) was carried out with respect to its origins, and involved the demolition of sub-standard additions to the original building. The interior has had ornamental plaster wall decorations added, made from original moulds.

Left: In the early 1990s, during an upgrade and refurbishment, the Town Hall had its main entrance blocked off and replaced with a new window of Deco design. This photograph shows it before the alterations were made.

In the mid-1930s, when Napier was largely rebuilt, the Streamline Moderne style became popular, especially for domestic architecture. It was a pleasing, uncluttered style with occasional Art Deco decoration, curvilinear rather than spiky. Walls were generally finished in stucco, and rounded bays or balconies were common features. Ranui Flats on the Marine Parade were designed and built by W J Green in 1938 - Napier's only example of a Streamline building on a large scale.

Following the uplifting of land after the earthquake, large areas of new land to the south of Napier became available for housing and the new suburb of Marewa was opened up in 1934. Many of Napier's best examples of Moderne style housing are to be found in this vicinity.

INDEX

GLOSSARY

Adobe — unfired, sun-dried brick, commonly used for building in Spain, Latin America and Western USA The adobe look was popular for Spanish Mission buildings, which were often plastered and painted white.

Bas-relief — sculpted figures or patterns which do not stand far out from the surface on which they are formed.

Bay — a vertical division in the exterior of a building marked by an arrangement of windows, pillars or roofing.

Campanario — a bell tower, a popular feature in the Spanish Mission style.

Capital — the head or crown of a column.

Casement — a window with the opening frame hung vertically. (By comparison, in a sash window, the frame slides vertically in grooves.)

Chevron — a moulding which forms a zigzag shape.

Coffering — a ceiling decoration consisting of sunken squares.

Comice — a projecting ornamental moulding along the top of a wall or arch.

Eaves — the underpart of a sloping roof overhanging a wall or verandah.

Espadana — a curved parapet at the top of a shaped gable.

Facing — the finish applied to the outer surface of a building.

Gable — the triangular upper portion of a wall at the end of a pitched roof.

Lintel — a horizontal beam or stone which bridges an opening.

Mosaic — surface decoration for walls, floors or steps formed of small pieces of glass, stone or marble.

Parapet — a low wall placed at the top of a house.

Pediment — the triangular (or segmental) upright front end of a moderately-pitched roof.

Pergola — a covered verandah made of wood or stone posts or pillars with open joists above, sometimes covered with climbing plants.

Pilaster — a shallow rectangular column projecting only slightly from a wall.

Scotia — a concave moulding.

Stucco — exterior plaster work often with a textured pattern.